THE MARRIAGE
DASHBOARD HANDBOOK

Written by Andy Savage

*To Amanda,
I am so glad you're my wife.
Andy*

The Marriage Dashboard Handbook
Copyright © 2016 Andy Savage

Requests for information should be addressed to:
Andy Savage Ministries | AndySavage.com | @andysavage
Highpoint Church | HighpointMemphis.com | @hpmemphis

Noted scripture quotations are taken from the *Holy Bible, The Holy Bible, English Standard Version*®. *ESV*®. copyright © 2001 by Crossway Bibles, a publishing ministry of Good News Publishers. Used by permission. All rights reserved. *The New International Version*®. *NIV*®. copyright © 1973, 1978, 1984 by International Bible Society. Used by permission of Zondervan. All rights reserved.

Emphases in scripture quotations have been added by the author.

All rights reserved. No part of this publication may be reproduced, stored in a retrieval system, or transmitted in any form or by any means—electronic, mechanical, photocopying, recording, or any other—except for brief quotations in printed reviews, without the prior permission of the author.

*Cover design and interior layout by Meredith Browndyke Smith.
Edited by Kelly Langley, Jessica Seidner, Melissa Wadsworth, and Becky Gabriel.
Printed in the United States of America.*

TABLE OF CONTENTS

Page 1   Introduction

Page 3   The AHA Moment

Page 4   The Marriage Dashboard Assessment Tool

Page 6   Part 1 : Start with God

Page 20   Part 2 : Have Fun Together

Page 34   Part 3 : Honor Each Other

Page 48   Part 4 : Live in Community

Page 62   Part 5 : Fight for Intimacy

Page 76   Small Group Leader Guide Discussion Questions

Page 83   Additional Resources

INTRODUCTION

I am notorious for my total disregard for the warning lights on my car's dashboard. I blame my bad habit on the fact that I drove a 1997 Ford Explorer, affectionately known as "The Exploder," for more than 16 years. I guess I became so accustomed to the growing list of unidentified noises, randomly occurring warning lights and gauges that just quit working that I became numb to them. Ignoring the warning signs, of course, always caught up with me and resulted in unfortunate and often expensive problems.

Ignoring warning signs is the unfortunate reality of far too many marriages. Couples grow so accustomed to each other that they slowly become numb to the warning lights begging them to do some much-needed maintenance on their marriages. This is so common our society has coined phrases for it such as, "the seven year itch" or "midlife crisis." Time and neglect have their way, and marital satisfaction declines while marriage frustrations rise. The list of problems continues to grow as does the cost of repairing those problems. At some point, many couples convince themselves that the cost of replacement is less expensive and may be less painful than repair.

I have seen this slow, downward trend take out more marriages than you can imagine. But here's the truth: It doesn't have to be this way. There is a way to have a strong, growing, God-honoring marriage for a lifetime, which is why I developed the Marriage Dashboard. It dawned on me one day that automakers realized a long time ago that providing the car owner with some basic information in a user-friendly format greatly improved the chances for the safe and long-term operation of the vehicle. So I developed a Marriage Dashboard to give couples like you a simple way to evaluate the current state of your marriage and information to help you make some needed adjustments for the safe and long-term operation of your marriage. By regularly checking the status of these five marriage gauges, you can better understand what areas of your marriage are running smoothly and what areas may need a little maintenance. As you read through this book, you will see a specific gauge icon for each section to help you stay focused and engaged on growth in that particular area of your marriage.

This book is designed to give you the opportunity to improve your marriage. But it is not Love Potion #9 or a gimmick. I cannot guarantee that going through this book will save a fledgling marriage. However, the principles you will find on these pages have been tested by hundreds of couples—and they work! Working through this book can be a game-changer when couples agree to give the process their best efforts and depend on God for help. The optimal environment for this study is a small group or Sunday school class. When you have others with you on the journey, it radically improves the outcome. So before you drive your marriage off a cliff, do the one thing you should have done long ago—check your dashboard.

THE AHA MOMENT

At the end of every reading, you will be invited to "Reflect & Respond" to the content you have read. One of those opportunities is, "List your AHA moment from today's reading." The idea is to keep a record of key statements, thoughts or convictions that emerge as you are reading and meditating on God's truth. These AHA moments will be extremely valuable as you continue to grow in your marriage.

Before you begin, I would like to offer a prayer for you.

Heavenly Father, thank You for the marriage on the other side of this book. I pray You give the husband or wife reading this prayer the courage to be honest, diligent and dependent upon You. I pray You speak clearly through every line they read and You guide every conversation birthed from this book. Strengthen this marriage. Grant them the gift of faith, the gift of repentance and the love of Christ wherever it is needed. Protect, sustain and bring them more joy together in the coming years than all the previous years. God, would You use this marriage for Your glory. May this watching world see You in them. Thank You for displaying Your great love for us through Your Son, Jesus. May this couple share that love with one another for the rest of their lives.

In the name of Jesus I pray, AMEN.

Andy Savage
Amanda's Husband; Dad to Drew, Cooper, Wesley, Ford and Joshua
Teaching Pastor, Highpoint Church, Memphis, Tenn.

THE MARRIAGE DASHBOARD ASSESSMENT TOOL

Welcome to the Marriage Dashboard!
The image you see below contains what I like to call the "Five Gauges of Married Life." Each gauge represents a specific indicator of health in marriage. I believe consistent attention, evaluation and improvement in these five areas of your relationship will help you develop a marriage that truly becomes stronger over time.

After reading the introduction to each section of this book, you will take a moment to conduct a basic evaluation of your marriage using the specific gauge for each chapter. Individually, using a simple scale of "1-10", rate where you feel your marriage ranks. This simple evaluation will help you approach each section with intentionality and focus.
No matter where your marriage falls on the gauge, there is always room for improvement.

START WITH GOD | HAVE FUN TOGETHER | HONOR EACH OTHER | LIVE IN COMMUNITY | FIGHT FOR INTIMACY

START WITH GOD

I believe God invented marriage and His word is the standard by which we are to conduct married life. The Start with God gauge in the Marriage Dashboard measures our willingness to trust God in marriage, which means we must deny ourselves and align with His plan.

PART I : START WITH GOD

As you begin the journey of strengthening your marriage, it is vital to start in the right place. Most people, if they are honest, agree they have room to grow in their marriage. You do not have to be on the edge of divorce to recognize your marriage relationship could benefit from some improvements. When it comes to improving your marriage, if you are anything like me, you tend to begin by thinking about your own selfish desires. It is easy to believe your marriage will improve by getting your way. However, selfishness wars against the fundamental reality of strong marriages—oneness. God's plan is for you and your spouse to be unified, or what the Bible refers to as being "one flesh" (Genesis 2:24). Selfishness creates a major barrier to building unity and oneness. Starting with you only leads to more problems.

Conversely, you might choose an equally damaging, but seemingly more noble approach. Instead of starting with self, you start with your spouse. Sounds better, doesn't it? After all, you are choosing not to be selfish. However, this approach is also flawed. Giving your spouse their way has a place, but not as a primary means of strengthening your marriage; it's not the place to start. You see, starting with your spouse simply means you are trading your selfishness for their selfishness. The result is predictable—you begin to resent your spouse!

By now you are probably putting two and two together. The only effective place to start the process of strengthening your marriage is, with God. He has a lot to say about love, romance and marriage. In fact, there's an entire book of the Bible dedicated to the subject, the Song of Solomon. God is your Creator and the Author of marriage and is therefore, the greatest source of wisdom on you, your spouse and this unique relationship He designed.

Starting with God means listening and obeying what He says about love, romance and marriage. It means deferring to God's way above your way (or your spouse's way, for that matter). There are two very important, yet practical, steps for you to take to start with God.

First, read God's word. This is how you hear the voice of God. Taking time to read God's word fills your mind with His wisdom and truth, which will help you make better decisions. In this book, you will be presented with God's word, specifically as it applies to marriage. Second, you must pray. Prayer is talking with God and asking Him for His help to do what His word says. Prayer is living in the reality of these two statements: "God, I'm not capable of loving my spouse as I should," and "God, show me how to love my spouse the way You love me." These prayers, combined with God's word, will invite God's wisdom into your life. As you start with God each day, you will begin to sense God leading you by bringing to your mind positive action steps that are in alignment with His word. Taking these steps will begin to strengthen your marriage. The real step of faith comes in when you follow God's lead by taking action and seeing what happens.

On the **START WITH GOD** gauge below, rate your marriage using a scale of 1-10.

START WITH GOD

Remember, this is your individual assessment. I encourage you to be honest and make any specific notes you would like to include or questions you have in the margin.

DAY 1 : "SEEK FIRST"

So do not worry, saying, 'What shall we eat?' or 'What shall we drink?' or 'What shall we wear?' For the pagans run after all these things, and your heavenly Father knows that you need them. But seek first His kingdom and His righteousness, and all these things will be given to you as well. Therefore do not worry about tomorrow, for tomorrow will worry about itself. Each day has enough trouble of its own.
(Matthew 6:31-34)

What is the first thing you do in the morning? I am just about worthless without some coffee in my system. My need for caffeine in the morning, along with my genuine love for coffee, drives me to ensure a hot cup of coffee is never more than a few minutes away from the moment I wake up every morning. Each night before bed, I make sure the coffee is set and ready so the only thing I have to think about is pouring my coffee into a cup.

Today, you start focusing on the first gauge on the Marriage Dashboard, Start with God. I truly believe success in marriage often boils down to establishing routines and habits around the important steps that strengthen your marriage. The first gauge, Start with God, means you must evaluate your starting point, especially in terms of your thoughts. Matthew 6:31-34 recognizes the temptation we all face to start with worry. "What shall we eat?" or "What shall we drink?" or "What shall we wear?" I'm doubtful many of you reading this are worried about those particular issues, but I am certain there are things you do worry about. What worries you in your marriage?

Countless marriages suffer because one spouse worries that if they start giving their best to the marriage, it would not be noticed, appreciated or even reciprocated. Jesus reminds you that worry only hijacks your faith in God. Can you imagine demoting your worry and giving laser-focused attention to God's word and God's ways? Seeking first God's kingdom and His righteousness means trusting God to supply everything you feel you need or want. It truly means allowing your faith and trust in God to drown your worries. It actually frees you to unconditionally give your best to your marriage. Seeking God first is the secret to building a strong, lasting and enjoyable marriage.

REFLECT & RESPOND:

1. What are your top three worries related to your marriage?

2. Are your worries based on facts or feelings? (If you have factual reasons for your worries, you may need to seek trusted counsel to help you establish a solid plan to rebuild trust in light of those issues.)

3. What good can come from giving less than your best to your marriage?

4. What routine do you have or need to have in your life to help you Start with God each day?

5. List your AHA moment from today's reading.

DAY 2 : "DON'T BE FOOLISH"

Are you so foolish? After beginning by means of the Spirit, are you now trying to finish by means of the flesh?
(Galatians 3:3)

Marriage is not simply a human institution. It is easy to look at marriage through the lens of the mechanics of marriage, such as good communication, spending time together, sharing common interests, mutual attraction and companionship. While no one questions the importance of these "marital mechanics," you must remember, marriage is first and foremost a union defined and established by God, making marriage somewhat mysterious. Certainly, marriage is greatly affected by the mechanics of the relationship and the practicality of life together; however, marriage also involves the invisible, but very real, presence of God's Spirit.

Jesus highlighted this fact in Matthew 19:6 when He said, "Therefore what God has joined together, let no one separate." Jesus emphasized the reality that God plays a critical role in joining a husband and wife together in marriage. In fact, it is safe to say it is not enough to consider marriage a commitment simply between a man and a woman. God is a unique part of this union; He is what makes matrimony, holy matrimony.

The Apostle Paul challenges followers of Christ in Galatians 3 with a question, "After beginning by means of the Spirit, are you now trying to finish by means of the flesh?" What a powerful question! Wrestle with this question in your marriage. Of course, you need to work on the various mechanics of married life, but let's get first things first.
Are you trying to accomplish God's plan with human effort? This is why starting with God is so vital. When you operate with a willingness to obey God's word and submit to His ways in marriage, you experience God's power to change both you and your spouse in ways you could have never predicted or manufactured on your own. When we give God our attention, He has a way of making all those relationship mechanics work most effectively. Lastly, Paul adds insult to injury with his opening question, "Are you so foolish?" Paul considered it foolish to attempt to

live for Christ out of the flesh. This is one hundred percent true in marriage as well. It is foolish (and frankly, impossible) to pursue a God-honoring marriage in your flesh.

REFLECT & RESPOND:

1. Using a scale of 1–10, rank how focused you are on God's direction in your marriage and why?

2. Describe a time when you tried to manufacture marriage success without the guidance of God's Spirit?

3. What problem or issue do you need to table as you refocus on God's leading in your marriage?

4. What action can you take in your marriage today in response to the leading of God's Spirit? (You may need a moment to pray about this one.)

5. List your AHA moment from today's reading.

DAY 3 : "WHAT HAVE I GOTTEN MYSELF INTO?"

Create in me a pure heart, O God, and renew a steadfast spirit within me. (Psalm 51:10)

I tend to have a taste for adventure. On more occasions than I can count, my thrill-seeking personality has resulted in some very urgent prayers for God's help and protection. Whether skiing down a black diamond run in Colorado or getting ready to leap from an airplane on my first skydiving trip in Florida, I have had my fair share of "What have I gotten myself into, God help me!" prayers!

Does this sound like your marriage? I don't mean that offensively. You may be reading this book as part of God's answer to your "What have I gotten myself into, God help me!" prayer. Marriage can feel like this. God is not oblivious to our challenges and struggles in marriage. In fact, if you have had these secret questions in your soul, please know you are not alone. I've had them and lots of godly people have them. Marriage will push you to the limits of your selfishness. There will be days when you will have awful thoughts about your spouse and these thoughts will sometimes come out during an argument.

I love the heartbeat of Psalm 51. King David is writing these words as the one God called, "a man after God's own heart." Yes, even spiritual giants struggle. The passage represents David's honest prayer of bringing his struggle to God. First, he asked God to purify his heart. You may need this prayer today. Ask God to purify your heart from the negative and pessimistic thoughts toward your spouse. Ask God to weed out your selfishness and bring you back into alignment with His word. David then asked God to restore a steadfast spirit in him. You will need this prayer at some point in your marriage. Ask God to restore a spirit of commitment and loyalty in your marriage, first to God's plan and second to your spouse. You need God's help to stay faithful to your vows. You need God's help to weather the storms of marriage. You need God's help to love when you don't feel like loving.

Perhaps you feel embarrassed to admit your impure heart or your inconsistent spirit. Allow the truth of this scripture to free you from those fears, and invite God to bring a holy restoration into your marriage.

REFLECT & RESPOND:

1. In your marriage, what has been the cause for the "what have I gotten myself into" feelings?

2. What exists in the secrecy of your heart that needs to be purified? Would you consider sharing this with a trusted friend?

3. List two examples of how marriage has highlighted your selfishness.

4. Where in your marriage do you feel your commitment to God's plan wavering?

5. List your AHA moment from today's reading.

DAY 4 : "FALLING IN LOVE"

We love because He first loved us.
(1 John 4:19)

"I love you. I'm just not sure I'm IN love with you." I have heard this sad line many times from people who are trying to explain the reason they just cannot continue in their marriages. This sentiment has become comparable to adultery or abuse in some marriages today. It's as if "falling out of love" is the undeniable cue for a divorce. The trump-card statement sends a message that someone else, namely your spouse, is to blame for causing love to die. This forces some serious questions about love. Is love really that fragile? Is love something your spouse has to earn continually? Is love something you "fall" into, or is it something you choose?

I am a firm believer that love is a choice. However, I am not indifferent toward my emotions or immune to the realities of life's complexities, busyness, challenging circumstances or the relational wear and tear of marriage. Over the course of married life, love can certainly take a beating. However, like my granddad used to say, "It takes a lickin' and keeps on tickin'."

True love is far more durable than you might think. True love is not found in the movies or wherever the grass seems to be greener. True love has its source in God. 1 John 4 reveals the foundational truth that God is love and all true forms of love have their source in Him. Understanding this truth about love creates a radically different reality for those who know God personally through Jesus Christ. In fact, God's directives for His people to love come from their experiences with Him. In other words, we love best by experience. God's love is where we must start. When you experience God's perfect love, your well of love deepens.
To love your spouse well, don't start by demanding they meet all of your expectations. Instead, focus on God's love toward you and love your spouse in the same way.

Aren't you glad God does not require you to earn His love? You have been given the love of God because He is a God of love, not because you have performed well enough to earn it. You now have that same opportunity in your marriage. You can love your spouse because you draw from a limitless well of God's perfect love toward you. Romans 5:8 says, "But God demonstrates his own love for us in this: while we were still sinners, Christ died for us." Once and for all, God yanked the rug out from under your excuses. You do not have to wait until you feel like it. You do not have to always get your way. Your spouse does not have to be perfect. You love because He first loved you.

REFLECT & RESPOND:

1. What are some of the excuses you have used to withhold your love from your spouse?

2. What is the difference between being "in love" and choosing love?

3. Make a list of 10 words that describe God's love toward you.

4. What is one step you can take today to show love to your spouse, irrespective of their attitude or actions?

5. List your AHA moment from today's reading.

DAY 5 : "THE SQUIRREL"

If any of you lacks wisdom, you should ask God, who gives generously to all without finding fault, and it will be given to you. But when you ask, you must believe and not doubt, because the one who doubts is like a wave of the sea, blown and tossed by the wind. That person should not expect to receive anything from the Lord. Such a person is double-minded and unstable in all they do.
(James 1:5-8)

My commute to work each day involves driving the first five to six miles down a few winding, rural roads. These roads are beautiful, but they come with hazards. It is common after storms to find limbs and occasionally entire trees across the road. I have lost valuable time stuck behind a large tractor owned by one of the farmers in the area. By far, the most dangerous and frustrating hazard is the squirrels. It never fails that I end up in a game of chicken with the squirrel in the middle of the road. I always end up yelling at the squirrel to move so I don't run over him. Inevitably, the squirrel starts going left, then seems to question his judgment and darts to the right, only to question the merits of going right and here he comes left again. Meanwhile, I'm yelling, "MOVE!"

Do you ever feel like a squirrel in your relationship with God? I think the analogy is more accurate than we care to admit. James 1 reveals an essential step in starting with God—asking for His wisdom. This sometimes difficult step starts with humility. You must have the humility to admit that you lack wisdom. I have learned through my ministry coaching many couples over the years that when someone blames their spouse for a problem, they effectively turn off God's wisdom in their life. It is easy to assess problems with blame, but that is not the path to wisdom. God loves to give wisdom to those who admit they need it and to those who ask for it.

James reveals what it looks like to lack in wisdom. You are like the waves of the sea, blown and tossed by the wind. You become double-minded and unstable. You start acting like the squirrel who can't decide to go left or right. God's plan is to protect you and to provide His best for you through His wisdom activated in your life. This is essential for a God-honoring marriage. God wants you to live with the confidence and stability that comes from His wisdom. He wants to spare you from a fickle and wishy-washy marriage. Your marriage needs the stabilizing force of God's wisdom, but there's a catch: You must believe and not doubt (v6). What does this mean? It means applying God's wisdom to your life. It means doing things God's way, not your own way. It means you stop evaluating and questioning God's word and start obeying God's word. Obedience to God's word is the only real test of God's wisdom in your life and marriage.

REFLECT & RESPOND:

1. What is the most pressing need for wisdom in your marriage today?

2. What problems or issues have you been blaming on your spouse?

3. Describe what you think double-mindedness looks like in a marriage.

4. Draft a simple prayer admitting your need for God's wisdom and your commitment to obeying God's word in your marriage.

5. List your AHA moment from today's reading.

HAVE FUN TOGETHER

I believe every couple needs to prioritize activities and experiences that foster a sense of fun in the relationship. Fun, laughter and good memories are often overlooked as components of a thriving marriage. The Have Fun Together gauge on the Marriage Dashboard measures the current level of fun you have together as a couple.

PART 2 : HAVE FUN TOGETHER

Growing old together does not mean growing bored together!
Do you and your spouse regularly have fun? When was the last time you laughed—really laughed—together? Sometimes while perusing social media, my wife and I will notice "that couple" who always seems to do the coolest things together. Whether it be concerts, quick day trips, exotic vacations or creative at-home date nights, they always seem to be having fun. Inevitably, we turn to one another and say, "We need to have more fun!"

God intends for your marriage to be enjoyed, not simply endured.
I have yet to meet a couple who got married with dreams of mediocrity. However, many marriages end up there. Marriage devolves from something full of excitement to something endured. It takes intentional effort to have fun in marriage. The reality is, the longer you are married, the more complex your life becomes with career pressures, children, church commitments and so on. It seems the one thing that always gets cut from the schedule is fun. Never underestimate the importance of fun. Having fun in your marriage is like putting fuel in the tank of romance. Having fun together can raise your appreciation for one another and develop greater levels of intimacy because of the insights you gain from sharing those moments. Every positive experience a couple shares helps to build and strengthen their connection.

It's important to remember that no matter how much you envy your friends on social media, having fun is not a "one size fits all" proposition. Having fun together requires you to study your spouse and communicate with each other to determine what fun looks like in your season of life. We have some friends who filled a mason jar with 52 date night ideas they would enjoy doing together. Each week, they randomly select one idea. This is a plan that works for them in their stage of life. One date night a week simply may not work for everyone. Having fun together does not require spending lots of money. Having fun together should be a priority for every marriage, regardless of income or economic status.

Like all things in married life, selfishness will be your enemy. Couples often drift apart because they selfishly pursue separate interests to the degree they stop building essential connections. You and your spouse may have to experiment with ideas in order to discover or create connecting points in your marriage. This will likely take some compromise and a little trial and error, but the effort is worth it. The first step may simply be to look at your spouse and say out loud that you would like to begin the quest of rediscovering fun in your marriage.

On the **HAVE FUN TOGETHER** gauge below, rate your marriage using a scale of 1–10.

HAVE FUN TOGETHER

Remember, this is your individual assessment. I encourage you to be honest and make any specific notes you would like to include or questions you have in the margin.

DAY 1 : "REJOICE"

May your fountain be blessed,
and may you rejoice in the wife of your youth.
A loving doe, a graceful deer—
may her breasts satisfy you always,
may you ever be intoxicated with her love.
(Proverbs 5:18-19)

I am a sucker for videos of servicemen and servicewomen returning home. I especially love when the setup is a total surprise to the child at school or the spouse at work or the family at some community event. I cannot help but get emotional. There is a reason these videos so often go viral—people intuitively understand the longing to be with those they love.

King Solomon wrote many of the Proverbs we love and quote. He was uniquely gifted by God with wisdom. In Proverbs 5:18-19, he reminds the reader to rejoice in marriage. I know that word "rejoice" seems like a word your grandmother might use or something you might hear in a Christmas pageant somewhere; however, this word is actually a powerful discipline in romance. Discipline isn't usually the first thing that comes to mind when you think of romance, but there is genius in this concept. Rejoicing in marriage means focused attention. The reason there is such rejoicing when a soldier returns home is because there was intense and exclusive focus on that person that became a longing fulfilled upon their return. Solomon suggests you apply that same intense and exclusive focus toward your spouse. It means disciplining yourself to reserve your deepest joy for your spouse. It is this discipline that produces the fulfilling marriage you long to experience.

Verse 19 is a rather eye-opening look into the marriage of a couple that rejoices with one another. The call to "rejoice in the wife of your youth" indicates this couple is well beyond the honeymoon phase; however, they are fully enjoying one another. They are "intoxicated" with love for each other. How does this happen in marriage? A marriage with this depth of enjoyment comes from the discipline, decision and habit of rejoicing.

REFLECT & RESPOND:

1. Do you agree that romance needs discipline? Why or why not?

2. In what ways might you improve your "focused attention" in your marriage?

3. What are the top three distractions robbing your romantic focus from your spouse?

4. Describe the last time you truly rejoiced in your spouse. Consider sharing that memory with them and expressing your desire to rejoice in them.

5. List your AHA moment from today's reading.

DAY 2 : "ROMANTIC PLAYFULNESS"

When the men of the place asked him about his wife, he said, "She is my sister," for he feared to say, "My wife," thinking, "lest the men of the place should kill me because of Rebekah," because she was attractive in appearance.

When he had been there a long time, Abimelech king of the Philistines looked out of a window and saw Isaac laughing with Rebekah his wife. So Abimelech called Isaac and said, "Behold, she is your wife. How then could you say, 'She is my sister'?" Isaac said to him, "Because I thought, 'Lest I die because of her.'"
(Genesis 26:7–9)

No matter how many times I read the Bible, I continue to be blown away by truths and insights I have never noticed. I suppose that is what you can expect from a book inspired by the God of the universe! Genesis 26:7-9 is one of those passages. I discovered this passage as I was doing one of those "read through the Bible in a year" programs. The context is this: Isaac and his wife, Rebekah, are fleeing a famine in their homeland and settling in the land of Gerar, a place ruled by the Philistines. Out of fear that the Philistine king, Abimelech, would kill him to acquire Rebekah as his own wife, Isaac lies and claims Rebekah is his sister. Isaac made a foolish move, but it sets up a very important marriage principle.

King Abimelech happens to see Isaac and Rebekah from his window, unbeknownst to Isaac and Rebekah. Verse 8 records what the king sees, "Abimelech king of the Philistines looked out of a window and saw Isaac laughing with Rebekah his wife." The Hebrew word here is "tsachaq," meaning to laugh, sport or play. Isaac and Rebekah are being playful with each other. Their playfulness is obviously romantic. The king calls Isaac and confronts the lie. In other words, there was no question in the king's mind that Isaac and Rebekah were actually husband and wife. Why? Simply put, because they were having fun together.

Having fun together is much more than doing "fun" things. There is a type of romantic playfulness that is reserved for the one person you call husband or wife. It is more than the fun you have with friends.

I believe God wants you to have a marriage full of laughter, fun and romantic playfulness. It is possible to have a marriage that leaves no question to the watching world whether the two of you are married.

REFLECT & RESPOND:

1. List the name of a couple you know that displays the "romantic playfulness" highlighted in Genesis 26.

2. What are three examples of romantic playfulness you enjoy with your spouse?

3. What are three examples of romantic playfulness your spouse enjoys with you?

4. How will you initiate romantic playfulness this week with your spouse?

5. List your AHA moment from today's reading.

DAY 3 : "BE CONSIDERATE"

Husbands, in the same way be considerate as you live with your wives, and treat them with respect as the weaker partner and as heirs with you of the gracious gift of life, so that nothing will hinder your prayers.
(1 Peter 3:7)

I have always been a bit of an adrenaline junky. When I was growing up, I jumped at the chance to try things that forced me to push through my fears to discover the fun on the other side. Now, as a father, I love giving my kids those same opportunities. However, my children do not always share the same taste for adventure as their old man. I have learned what I considered fun at their age may not be fun for them. This principle holds true in marriage as well. Having fun together can absolutely strengthen the marriage bond; however, the goal is not simply that one of you has fun. The goal is to have fun together. Marriage is full of such compromises.

In 1 Peter 3, husbands are challenged to, "be considerate as you live with your wives, and treat them with respect." This verse illustrates the pathway to a deeper, more meaningful connection in marriage. God instructs every husband to think about the security, well-being and enjoyment of his wife. There is humility and grace in this approach. Just like my desire to entice my kids to become adrenaline junkies feels forced and uncomfortable to them, in marriage, demanding fun and connection solely on your terms is rarely well-received.

God always has a purpose in the path He designs. Through being considerate and showing respect, the lines of communication open and true connection becomes possible. This is such an important facet to a healthy marriage that God reveals that failing to do so hinders your prayers! While this may seem like a severe consequence, it actually makes sense. Failing to be considerate and show respect for your spouse is essentially saying to God, "I know better than You, and I will do things my way." The very attitude that refuses to show consideration and respect toward your spouse is the same attitude that does not seek God in prayer.

Husbands, there is a deeper and more enjoyable connection available with your wife—and for that matter, with God—through a commitment to show consideration and respect. Wives, of course, should not become passive in marriage based on this truth. Instead, you should always give your best and seek a connection with your husband.

REFLECT & RESPOND:

1. Husbands, do a quick search online of the definition of the word "considerate" and write down what you find. Based on the definition, grade yourself on how considerate you are toward your wife.

2. Wives, grade your husband on being considerate of you. In addition, grade your attitude in response to your husband.

3. Husbands, make a list of three ways you can improve in being considerate of your wife.

4. Wives, make a list of three ways you will refuse to be passive and actively pursue connection with your husband.

5. List your AHA moment from today's reading.

DAY 4 : "THE PAYOFF"

The heart of her husband trusts in her,
and he will have no lack of gain.
She does him good, and not harm,
all the days of her life.
(Proverbs 31:11-12)

The hardest part of any investment is waiting for the return, which requires great patience. Marriage is the same way. Every good decision, every act of love and every kind word contribute to an ever-increasing sense of value in the relationship. In Proverbs 31, we find the famous chapter about an amazing wife, the "Proverbs 31 woman." What we often overlook, though, is that this passage is actually a husband praising his wife, even doting on her, after years of life together. The joy and love he displays for his wife throughout the chapter indicates how much he values her.

Having fun together is much more than sharing a few hobbies or fun activities. Having fun together means consistently investing in the good of your marriage over time. It means experiencing growth in your marriage. Allow me to state the obvious: marriage is no fun if there is no growth. You both expect the other to continually grow and improve. Proverbs 31:11-12 reveals the payoff of continued growth and improvement in a marriage.

Initially, we see trust is fully established. When you commit to continually grow in your faith and in your marriage, you engender trust with your spouse. Trust is the currency of relationships. Nothing makes marriage more fun than knowing you can trust one another. Trust eliminates any questions of motives or commitment.

Next, we see "he will have no lack of gain." This husband is so blessed by his wife that he perceives no lack of gain. He feels like he "has it all" because of her. There is no fear that he has missed out on someone or something else. There is no regret in his marriage.

Lastly, "She does him good, and not harm, all the days of her life."

He has experienced enough of a consistent track record with his wife that he can forecast a future defined by good and not harm. He has absolutely no question of her value. He only sees her as a source of goodness.

This kind of payoff does not happen by accident. It requires you to faithfully invest in your marriage every day. It means making the next right decision and fighting the temptations that distract you from seeking the good of your marriage. If this becomes your commitment in marriage, you will look up one day and discover that your marriage is rich with value. You will be able to brag on your wife or husband much like we read in Proverbs 31.

REFLECT & RESPOND:

1. Make a list of four or five reasons why you are grateful for your spouse.

2. Where do you need to be patient with the growth of your spouse?

3. Are you committed to personal growth for the good of your marriage? If no, why not?

4. What decisions are you currently making to build a track record of trustworthiness?

5. List your AHA moment from today's reading.

DAY 5 : "FUN SEX"

Come, my beloved,
let us go out into the fields
and lodge in the villages;
let us go out early to the vineyards
and see whether the vines have budded,
whether the grape blossoms have opened
and the pomegranates are in bloom.
There I will give you my love.
(Song of Solomon 7)

The Song of Solomon is a very interesting book of the Bible. Just read the first few verses, and you will see why many scholars believe Hebrew boys were not allowed to read it until their Bar Mitzvahs or coming of age ceremonies. Solomon, the writer, is believed to have written more than 1,000 songs and considered this one greater than all of them. Hence the song is named the Song of Solomon. or sometimes, the Song of Songs. The text is sensual, deeply romantic and even erotic, yet at the same time absolutely within the scope of holy scripture, believed to be without error and written by the inspiration of the Holy Spirit. It was considered a handbook of sorts on marriage for the Israelites. This may seem a bit surprising because so few marriages today remotely resemble the kind of love, romance, sensuality and pure enjoyment outlined in the Song of Solomon.

In Song of Solomon 7, we see a clear example of this enjoyment. The female character in this story calls her lover (husband) to join her in the fields, to go out early in the vineyards where she will give him her love. I know husbands who would faint if their wives suggested such an outdoor adventure! This is clearly a couple having fun together in the most intimate way. This is part of God's plan. It is right and good for married couples to fully and creatively enjoy one another in every sense of the word. In fact, I believe it is fair to interpret the Song of Solomon, as well as other Biblical texts such as 1 Corinthians 7:1–5, as God's total endorsement of full sexual expression enjoyed in the context of a loving, respectful and honorable marriage. As surprising as it may be to you, God is not a prude. He is not against sex. He actually invented the whole idea and gave it to couples as an exclusive and mutually enjoyable gift to marriage.

Many couples struggle to share the kind of enjoyment described in this passage of scripture. Perhaps you need to initiate a conversation about how to better communicate around your sexual relationship. Take this opportunity to rethink your expectations and even ask God to restore a proper view of sexuality, designed by God to be a source of love, romance, sensuality and pure enjoyment.

REFLECT & RESPOND:

1. List five words that describe your current view of sex in your marriage.

2. How do you feel about the idea that the Bible contains a book like the Song of Solomon?

3. Do you feel your current sexual relationship in your marriage fits the description "a source of love, romance, sensuality and pure enjoyment?" Why or why not?

4. Do you and your spouse have an open line of communication around your sexual relationship? If not, would you be willing to initiate the dialogue?

5. List your AHA moment from today's reading.

HONOR EACH OTHER

I believe honor is the atmosphere of great marriages. Honor means elevating your spouse by choosing love, respect and grace. The Honor Each Other gauge measures the current level of honor in the way you speak and act toward each other.

PART 3 : HONOR EACH OTHER

Honor. You know it when you see it, but if you were asked to define it, you might not know where to start. Honor is the virtue behind why we stand to attention during the National Anthem. It is why we attend funerals and why we try to be on time for appointments. Honor can be defined as the collective quality of our character. Disrespect, dishonesty and rudeness have no place among honorable people or marriages.

It is likely the word honor made an appearance on your wedding day. "To love, honor, trust and serve from this day forward...." Honor is a basic expectation of the marriage, relationship. You want to be treated with honor in your marriage and so does your spouse. Honor has become an endangered relational trait today. Think about your last conflict with each other. Everything from our tone of voice to our body language to the words we choose to throw at our spouse can often cross the line of honor.

God wants to help you develop a marriage of honor. Honoring each other is not as complicated as it sounds. Think encouragement, communication and good manners. Honor will cause you to seek out ways to lift up and encourage. Honor is when we go above and beyond in our communication, not out of obligation, but out of respect. Honor means keeping your word, even when it's hard. Honor means keeping your marriage vows both externally and in the privacy of your mind. Honorable people use good manners by seasoning interactions with gracious words such as, "Thank you," "Please," and "You're welcome." Honor means refusing to demean, ignore or be rude toward your spouse. Honor means never intentionally criticizing or embarrassing your spouse, especially in front of others.

Honor believes the best first and elevates the good whenever possible. Honorable marriages are always made up of a husband and wife who are proud to be married to one another. Every marriage could benefit from a fresh commitment to honor each other.

A great first step would be to honor your spouse through intentional attempts to give encouragement, clear communication and good manners.

On the **HONOR EACH OTHER** gauge below, rate your marriage using a scale of 1-10.

HONOR EACH OTHER

Remember, this is your individual assessment. I encourage you to be honest and make any specific notes you would like to include or questions you have in the margin.

DAY 1 : "HEALING WORDS"

The words of the reckless pierce like swords, but the tongue of the wise brings healing.
(Proverbs 12:18)

My wife and I are very different, especially in the way we handle our words. My wife is a very thoughtful and deliberate communicator. She rarely speaks unless she has thoroughly thought through her words. I am the exact opposite. I tend to speak in order to discover what I'm thinking. For whatever reason, my thoughts crystallize when I speak them. This quality can be good if I am asked to give an extemporaneous speech, but it can be very bad in relationships. Just like me, I'm sure you are no stranger to the damage words can do.

Proverbs 12:18 is a powerful reminder of the impact of our words. As you focus on what it means to honor each other, it is important to recognize your speech is often the first place honor is felt in your marriage.
Your marriage will rise and fall by the words you say and even the words you fail to say. The scripture exhorts you to be careful with your words and not to be reckless. Reckless speech often can be well-intentioned. I have personally made the mistake of being reckless in my words because I was trying to be funny or tease my wife. Honor demands a higher standard regarding the words we choose. The sense of honor in your marriage will immediately increase by simply eliminating reckless speech.

The flip side is intentionally speaking good and wise words to your spouse. The scripture says, "the tongue of the wise brings healing." Many people carry painful wounds because of the words carelessly and recklessly spoken by their spouses. It is true that you cannot un-speak your words. However, God gives you a way to redeem and heal the damage you have caused. You have the opportunity today to bury the reckless and damaging speech of the past with an apology and a commitment to replace the bad with wise, good and healing words. Make the decision right now to bless your spouse with your speech.

REFLECT & RESPOND:

1. Who speaks the most healing and encouragement to you in your life?

2. Ask God to bring to mind any reckless words you have spoken to your spouse, and write down your plan to "bury" the reckless and damaging speech of the past.

3. Would you describe your speech toward your spouse as more damaging or healing? Why?

4. Make a list of three key messages your spouse needs to hear from you.

5. List your AHA moment from today's reading.

DAY 2 : "THE F-WORD"

Bear with each other and forgive one another if any of you has a grievance against someone. Forgive as the Lord forgave you. (Colossians 3:13)

I will never forget the day my oldest son came home from school and asked me what the "F-word" meant. I almost fell out of my chair. Apparently, another kid at school had discovered this word and began sharing his new found knowledge with his peers. Hoping my son was talking about some other word, I asked him, "What word are you talking about?" I cannot repeat his answer in this book, but it had four letters and rhymed with "duck." There's just something about that word. It's undoubtedly the strongest of all profanities. There is another "F-word" that carries a similar if not greater force—"forgiveness".

Forgiveness is a word that can stir up a deep longing in the heart of the one who has done wrong. Forgiveness can also stir up anger and resentment in the heart of the one who has been wronged. I have met people who have been in tears, begging a loved one for forgiveness only to be rejected. Likewise, I have met people who have questioned the audacity of me to suggest that they forgive someone who wronged them. Forgiveness is a polarizing word.

Marriage is fertile ground for forgiveness. The Apostle Paul writes these powerful words to the Colossians, "Forgive as the Lord forgave you." Paul is suggesting the standard of forgiveness in human relationships be the forgiveness you receive from Jesus Christ, which is radical forgiveness. The question is not, "Will your spouse fail or do wrong?" Of course they will! The question is, "Will you choose to forgive your spouse when they do?"

Forgiveness is one of the highest honors you can give your spouse. It is a powerful statement of your love that you would not hold a failure against them. Forgiveness and trust are not the same thing. Forgiveness opens the door to rebuilding trust. Forgiveness cancels any sense of debt your spouse owes you because of their failure. And only forgiveness can initiate the process of rebuilding trust based on genuine repentance before God for the sins that have been committed. Trust is restored when a proven track record of faithfulness emerges, producing confidence that real change has occurred and the same sin does not have the chance to continually damage your marriage.

REFLECT & RESPOND:

1. Do you consider yourself someone who is quick to forgive or someone who is slow to forgive? Why?

2. Make a list of the top five sins God has forgiven in your life.

3. Are there any sins you have committed that you want your spouse to forgive? Are there any sins your spouse has committed that you have not forgiven?

4. In your own words, describe the difference in forgiveness and trust.

5. List your AHA moment from today's reading.

DAY 3 : "THE GREATEST COMPLIMENT"

An excellent wife who can find?
She is far more precious than jewels.
(Proverbs 31)

There I was in the den reading a book when I heard commotion in the kitchen. It was clearly a parenting moment when my wife was correcting some act of terror committed by one of my boys. I overheard her say, "Do you see your father acting like this? Watch your father and act like him!" I was floored. She definitely did not say it for my benefit, but I heard it. I did not know it was possible to feel both extremely humble and proud at the same time, but I did. My wife told my son to be like me. Holding me up as an example for my boys to follow is the single greatest compliment I have ever received, and she didn't even mean to give it!

A compliment is powerful. The impact of a compliment increases exponentially based on the depth of the relationship. The people who know us best see both our strengths and weaknesses. When they give a compliment, they have filtered out the weaknesses and still see strength. A compliment is one of the highest honors you can give your spouse.

In Proverbs 31, the writer says, "An excellent wife who can find? She is far more precious than jewels." This is a major compliment. He is bragging on the goodness of his wife. His question, "An excellent wife who can find?" indicates the reality of life in a fallen world. There are so few people who work hard to be a good husband or wife, they are simply hard to find. They are just like a rare treasure, and he found one. He values his wife above even financial wealth.

Honor is found in two forms in this passage of scripture. First, the excellent wife honors her marriage by giving her best to her husband and family. Second, we see the husband acknowledge her excellence with the highest compliment. What a beautiful combination. You have the opportunity to honor each other by giving your best to your marriage, no matter what, as well as recognizing the excellence your spouse brings into your life. Both are incredible acts of honor.

REFLECT & RESPOND:

1. What is the best compliment you have ever received?

2. What changes do you need to make to honor your spouse by giving your best to your marriage?

3. List three compliments for your spouse that represent the blessing they bring into your life.

4. In what way does your spouse appreciate receiving compliments (in writing, spoken in public, spoken in private, etc.)?

5. List your AHA moment from today's reading.

DAY 4 : "ME-FIRST MENTALITY"

Wisdom's instruction is to fear the Lord, and humility comes before honor.
(Proverbs 15:33)

Children love to be first. I see this virtually every day in our family. It does not seem to matter what we are doing—as long as it promises to be positive, they fight to be first. First to get dessert. First to open Christmas presents. First to get Daddy's attention after work. First. First. First. Whoever gets the coveted first place celebrates, while the others pout, complain and melt down. Sometimes, it would just be nice if they would be a little more agreeable about sometimes being second, third, fourth or fifth.

Truthfully, the desire to be first is hardwired into humanity. It's called pride or arrogance or the "me-first" mentality. We all desperately want to be first, and this attitude follows you into marriage. The me-first mentality looks different now that you have grown up, but do not be fooled. It is the same basic pride that has plagued humanity since the dawn of time. In marriage, the me-first mentality causes you to become a competitor with your spouse instead of a teammate. You manipulate to get your way and pout, complain and shut down when you don't. Deep down, you have determined getting your way is evidence that you matter in the relationship. It is one of the ways you feel valued, respected and appreciated. It is a basic desire to be honored.

God offers a better way. Proverbs 15:33 reminds the reader, "fear the Lord, and humility comes before honor." Instead of fighting or manipulating to get your way, God invites you to fear Him. Fearing God means living with a genuine sense of reverence for Him. It is the kind of healthy fear that keeps you from going down the road of pride, arrogance or me-first. Additionally, God invites you to choose humility as your focus. Our sinful nature strives to be honored, but our Heavenly Father invites us to embrace humility as we trust in Him.

Walking away from the me-first mentality is no easy task. The more you surrender your "me-first" pride to God, the more closely connected you will be to Him. Along the way, your humility leaves an open door for your spouse to willingly and genuinely give you honor.

REFLECT & RESPOND:

1. Where in your marriage do you have a me-first mentality?

2. What is your default reaction when you don't get your way in your marriage?

3. How might you embrace humility in your marriage?

4. How do you feel about fearing the Lord and humbly leaving the door open for your spouse to honor you?

5. List your AHA moment from today's reading.

DAY 5 : "FORSAKING ALL OTHERS"

Let marriage be held in honor among all, and let the marriage bed be undefiled, for God will judge the sexually immoral and adulterous. (Hebrews 13:4)

I have performed hundreds of weddings. I truly love every opportunity to pronounce a couple husband and wife. Performing weddings has ruined me as far as simply attending weddings. I feel completely disconnected when I am not standing on the platform looking into the faces of the bride and groom. One of the reasons I love performing weddings is because I constantly revisit the marriage vows. These are some of the most important words two people will ever say to each other. One of the strongest statements within the marriage vows is, "forsaking all others." You probably said something very similar in your marriage vows. This simple phrase is a declaration that says, "I am giving you, my husband or wife, exclusive rights to my life. You have me in a way no one else has me."

This is the language of honor. The whole point behind the marriage vows is to elevate your commitment to the proper level of honor. Because of this, I do not perform weddings for couples who want to write their own vows. Marriage is God's domain. Marriage means coming together on God's terms, not your own terms. Hebrews 13:4 captures the heartbeat of marriage and reveals another example of the language of honor, "Let marriage be held in honor among all, and let the marriage bed be undefiled." The writer of Hebrews challenges the reader to see marriage through a lens of honor. One of the primary ways you honor marriage is to keep the marriage bed pure; you commit to "forsaking all others."

In society today, the "forsaking all others" commitment is up for grabs. There is no longer a strong commitment to keeping the marriage bed pure before or even during marriage. As a result, we see weak and fractured marriages as the new normal. One of the great threats to the vow of "forsaking all others" is the widespread availability of pornography. Use of pornography exists behind the lie that it isn't harmful because it isn't real or physical. Nothing could be further from the truth. Pornography, lust and fantasizing about another person is a dishonor to your spouse and to your marriage. In order to restore proper honor in marriage, we must return to this core statement of your marriage vows, "forsaking all others."

REFLECT & RESPOND:

1. Did you "keep the marriage bed pure" before marriage? Based on your answer, how did your purity decisions affect your marriage after the wedding day?

2. What healthy safeguards exist or need to be created in your life to support the vow of "forsaking all others"?

3. Make a list of any threats to purity currently in your life, such as pornography.

4. Draft a prayer renewing your commitment before God to "forsaking all others."

5. List your AHA moment from today's reading.

LIVE IN COMMUNITY

I believe every couple needs a set of friends to "do life with." No one out-swims the current of his or her closest friends. The Live in Community gauge on the Marriage Dashboard measures the presence of good friends in your life who encourage you to pursue a God-honoring marriage.

PART 4 : LIVE IN COMMUNITY

Over the years, I have met with hundreds of couples facing serious marriage trauma. In virtually every case, the damage could be filtered into two different categories: one or both people in the marriage either fell victim to isolation or negative influences. Isolation and negative influences are two sides of a very nasty coin. In fact, it is my belief that given enough time in either situation, some form of compromise will result that could seriously threaten the marriage relationship.

For much of my life, I tried and tried to create a regular habit of exercise, but failed time and again. The past few years, however, I have consistently exercised three to six times a week. Why the sudden change from inconsistency and frustration to consistency and growth? The single greatest factor for success has been a group of people committed to working out with me. I enlisted a community to support my goals. There is power when you live in community.

God's plan for your marriage is to live in community. The growth, the improvements and, ultimately, the joy you long for in marriage will benefit tremendously when you live in community. You cannot out-swim the current of your closest friends, and you will drown out on your own. Look just outside your marriage, who do you see? Are you surrounded by people who encourage or discourage your marriage? Are you alone? Living in community is more than simply having "married friends." You want to enlist a community committed to the same goals. Couples who are surrounded by a group of friends who are also seeking strong, God-honoring marriages tend to get caught up in that current. If you don't have this kind of community, your local church is the place to start.

Every married couple needs both strong and reliable couple friends, just as every married person needs strong and reliable friends who are allowed to speak directly into their lives. We cannot take lightly the temptations surrounding husbands and wives. Your community should provide much-needed accountability and encouragement as you journey through married life. To develop this sort of community, you must go beyond simply attending church or a small group. You will need to formalize these relationships so you and your community can share a common goal of strong, God-honoring marriages.

On the **LIVE IN COMMUNITY** gauge below, rate your marriage using a scale of 1–10.

LIVE IN COMMUNITY

Remember, this is your individual assessment. I encourage you to be honest and make any specific notes you would like to include or questions you have in the margin.

DAY 1: "THE PEOPLE WHO MAKE OR BREAK YOU"

Whoever walks with the wise becomes wise, but the companion of fools will suffer harm.
(Proverbs 13:20)

My greatest successes and failures in life share a common ingredient—the people around me. It is a law of nature: Your friends are truly the people who make or break you. As you read this, think about the five to 10 with whom you spend the most time. Is their net influence in your life positive or negative? I find this to be very telling when it comes to marriage health. In nearly every case of couples that wind up in my office in the middle of some sort of major marriage crisis, a common ingredient is missing—a lack of good friends, a lack of community.

The writer of the Proverbs understood the direct correlation between the outcomes in your life and the influences around you. There is an important phrase in Proverbs 13:20 to take notice of when understanding the importance of community: "walks with." This phrase is further clarified by the term "companion." These terms are essentially the same. The writer is referring to those people who become more than acquaintances. Your friends are the people who walk with you and join you as companions in life. They are the lasting people in your life. Why is this so important? God wants you to recognize that one of the primary ways you are influenced toward either wisdom or foolishness is found in the people who become friendship fixtures in your life.

If you want to grow in marriage wisdom, you must employ something greater than simply reading marriage books, blogs or attending church services. You must intentionally develop lasting friendships with those who exemplify wisdom, especially in the matters of marriage. Here's the catch—friendship takes time. You cannot microwave good friendships. You must journey through life together; you must "walk with" one another. It is in this process of "doing life together" that you begin to see your own life and marriage through the lens of those you trust. This helps give you perspective and keeps you from allowing your circumstances or emotions to get the best of you.

It is my belief that the vast majority of Christian adults sorely lack a community of strong, wisdom-producing and lasting friendships. To make things worse, developing this community in your life gets harder as you get older. With the demands of family obligations, work and the busyness of life, there simply is not the time to develop friendships like there was when you were younger. However, the reality remains, "Whoever walks with the wise becomes wise." Maybe it is time to sit down with your spouse and create an intentional plan to identify and develop a community of friends around your marriage.

REFLECT & RESPOND:

1. Who is the best friend you have ever had? Were they a positive or negative influence on you?

2. List the names of three people whose marriage you truly admire.

3. Are you in a season of life that is full of strong and positive friendships, or do you feel like your marriage is on an island?

4. List three ways you are going to increase your investment in developing friendships.

5. List your AHA moment from today's reading.

DAY 2 : "ENCOURAGEMENT"

And let us consider how to stir up one another to love and good works, not neglecting to meet together, as is the habit of some, but encouraging one another, and all the more as you see the Day drawing near. (Hebrews 10:24-25)

On occasion, I have a bout of discouragement in ministry. Not long ago, I faced one of those moments after meeting with a couple who was unhappy with our church. I attempted to address their concerns and reach a positive conclusion, all to no avail. I felt misunderstood, judged and discouraged because the couple was clearly unhappy and would likely leave our church in frustration. Literally, within minutes of leaving my office, I came face-to-face with a good friend who happened to be at the church at just the right time. I immediately shared my situation with him and, in my discouragement, he encouraged me. He spoke the truth about me to me. It is amazing how quickly I was thrown off balance by the frustrated couple and began to believe things about myself that simply are not true. I am extremely grateful for my friend.

The author of Hebrews is not shy to challenge the reader to embrace the power of community. These words about friendship are much like a user manual for healthy community. Friendship is not simply a passive title or status on social media. Friendship is an active role we play in one another's lives. Look at the specific elements of Christian community.

"Let us consider how to stir up one another to love and good works"
Healthy community means thinking about what your friends need before they ask. It means living with the knowledge that your friends depend on you to actively push them toward love and good works. Can you imagine the benefit for your marriage? We live in a society that loves to take the easy way out by saying, "It's none of my business," or "It's not my place." Nothing could be more false! Healthy community means speaking into the lives and marriages of your friends to "stir them up toward love and good works."

"Not neglecting to meet together"
Healthy community involves regular interaction. Friendship cannot

live on a shelf in your life. Godly friends become part of the routine. You must make time for each other. Carving out time with friends is essentially like giving them permission to give you feedback, counsel and encouragement.

"Encouraging one another"
Encouragement should define healthy community. Encouragement is important because discouragement is all too common. The average person reading this book is dealing with some level of discouragement. Unfortunately, the average person reading this book is also living with a deficit in healthy community. Do not underestimate the value of healthy community in your life. Healthy community is crucial to marriage because marriage is often the greatest potential source of discouragement.

REFLECT & RESPOND:

1. When was the last time you were discouraged and why?

2. Who do you call when the going gets tough?

3. Who in your life have you given permission to "stir up love and good works" in your marriage?

4. Who counts on you as part of their healthy community? Are you faithfully fulfilling Hebrews 10:24-25 toward them?

5. List your AHA moment from today's reading.

DAY 3 : "NOT SO EASILY CHANGED"

Iron sharpens iron, and one man sharpens another.
(Proverbs 27:17)

If you happened to drop in on me and the five other guys I work out with, it may shock you the way we talk to each other. No, I am not referring to the inappropriate humor that tends to come out of us. I am talking about the unfiltered way we coach each other. We challenge each other to push harder. We call out weakness when we see it. We correct bad form. We reprimand quitting too soon. And we utterly reject excuses. We have embraced the practice of "iron sharpening iron."

You likely have heard this phrase. The imagery is clear. It often takes an intense and violent process to sharpen iron. It's aggressive and harsh because iron is not easily changed. Hence, God uses this illustration to make His point. Healthy community involves the practice of iron sharpening iron. People are not changed easily. God uses those around us to make us better, which often requires intensity and honesty. It means calling it like you see it. It means caring enough about your friends that you are willing to be forthright.

I truly believe you need people around you who are close enough friends that they qualify as iron sharpening iron. And, by the way, not everyone qualifies. Among all those you call friends are a precious few who care enough to get past the superficial and engage the essential. They love you enough to hurt your feelings, if needed, in order to help you grow.

You are not changed easily. Friends who serve as iron in your life are a gift from God. Don't shy away; God intends to use them in your life to make you better.

REFLECT & RESPOND:

1. List three weaknesses in your life that negatively affect your marriage.

2. In light of your weaknesses, whom do you trust enough to be transparent with and to invite them in as "iron"?

3. What fears come to mind when you think about being transparent about your weaknesses?

4. What do you stand to gain in your marriage by inviting an iron sharpens iron friendship into your life?

5. List your AHA moment from today's reading.

DAY 4 : "CONFESSION"

Therefore confess your sins to each other and pray for each other so that you may be healed. The prayer of a righteous person is powerful and effective.
(James 5:16)

A disciple is a learner and follower of Jesus Christ. Discipleship is the word used to describe the process of helping someone grow as a disciple. Discipleship is anything but a solo sport. God uses people to make disciples (see Matthew 28:19-20). God leverages the maturity, spiritual gifts, strengths, talents and life experiences of one person to help promote growth in another. I truly believe a unique point of focus in discipleship is marriage. Literally, your marriage becomes a laboratory for fleshing out your faith and practicing the truths of God's word. In fact, I would go so far as to say, if your discipleship does not impact your marriage, it is only a facade.

Discipleship in marriage is one reason living in community is so vital. You simply cannot become all God wants you to become by yourself. James 5:16 is a famous passage that most of us try to avoid at all costs. God's word encourages you to confess your sins to each other. Immediately, the image comes to mind of sitting on the outside of the screen at the confessional spilling your guts to the priest who is safely and anonymously on the other side. Anonymous confession is not the intent of James 5:16. The context is friendship or community. God is encouraging disciples to have the courage to confess their sins to one another for the purpose of growth.

Everyone fears confession for the same reasons: judgment, rejection and embarrassment. However, God considers confession an essential part of discipleship and growth. The sins we struggle with only gain power in secrecy. When we confess our sins to a friend in the context of healthy community, we invite the power of God to heal us through their prayers. Do you have that sort of friend? There is nothing more defeating than trying to overcome your sin in your own strength. Because of your fears, your marriage will continue to suffer from the sins that trip you up. Your best intentions and promises to "never do that again" are only

Band-Aids. You need the power of community. You need a trusted friend to whom you can confess your sins and gain healing from their prayers.

REFLECT & RESPOND:

1. Do you consider yourself a disciple of Jesus Christ? If not, please talk to a trusted Christian friend or pastor to investigate what this means in your life.

2. Why is marriage a laboratory for discipleship?

3. Do you agree that your sins only gain power in secrecy? Why or why not?

4. Make a list of two or three secret sins you would like to overcome and the name of a trusted friend to whom you might confess them and seek prayer.

5. List your AHA moment from today's reading.

DAY 5 : "MARRIED WITH A PURPOSE"

Each of you should use whatever gift you have received to serve others, as faithful stewards of God's grace in its various forms. If anyone speaks, they should do so as one who speaks the very words of God. If anyone serves, they should do so with the strength God provides, so that in all things God may be praised through Jesus Christ. To Him be the glory and the power for ever and ever. Amen.
(1 Peter 4:10-11)

Recently, we gained a new neighbor. They happened to be a young couple who attends our church. They had no idea they moved down the street from us until I pulled into their driveway the day they moved in. The parents of the young man were relieved I was in the neighborhood. I think it gave them a sense of security and comfort. Since then, we wave in passing and stop to chat on occasion. On a recent trip out of town, I received a text message from my new neighbor who was driving by and noticed an unfamiliar car in our driveway. He was checking to make sure everything was okay. He is the only neighbor we have ever had who cared enough to do something like that. I realized, I am not just a good neighbor for him; he is also a good neighbor for me.

Living in community is not just something you receive—it is also something you give. Community is a two-way street. Obviously, it is easy to see what you stand to gain with good friends, yet there is just as much to give as there is to gain. It may surprise you to learn that you have something valuable to give others. There are people around you who need to benefit from the blessings God has given you. In fact, 1 Peter 4:10-11 makes it clear that "whatever gift you have" is for the purpose of serving others, not yourself.

Understanding this element of living in community will give your marriage a sense of purpose. I have approached dozens and dozens of couples with the idea of serving as marriage mentors to couples younger than them in age and in marriage. In many cases, you can see the timidity on their faces. At first, they feel unqualified for the task. Soon enough, they realize God uses their willingness and availability to serve in a powerful way to impact marriages for a lifetime.

God wants to use your experience as a couple to be a gift of grace to others. God wants to use your words and your actions in ways that represent His best for others. Your marriage is not just for your benefit. Who will be blessed because of your marriage?

REFLECT & RESPOND:

1. Do you believe you have valuable insights, experiences and gifts to offer others?

2. What keeps you from serving others and leveraging your marriage as a platform for God's grace through you?

3. Make a list of two or three couples around you who would benefit from your encouragement and investment.

4. Make a list of five to seven Biblical truths or principles about marriage you have learned that you might pass along to others.

5. List your AHA moment from today's reading.

FIGHT FOR INTIMACY

I believe intimacy is something worth fighting for; it takes intentionality and hard work. Intimacy describes the oneness couples share across all areas of their marriage relationship, from parenting and communication to finances and sex. The Fight for Intimacy gauge measures the current level of oneness in your marriage.

PART 5 : FIGHT FOR INTIMACY

Intimacy has been brilliantly defined as "being fully known and fully loved." That's a remarkable thought, isn't it? Can you imagine truly being fully known? The good, the bad and the ugly? For most people, that is a fearful thought. The fear of being fully known is the fear of rejection, judgment and being unwanted. God intends marriage to be a place where imperfect people are loved in the face of their imperfections. God wants marriage to be a place where true intimacy is not only established, but sustained.

Our culture often limits intimacy to sexual intimacy. True oneness and intimacy certainly involves sexual intimacy, but it is far more than sex. Intimacy in marriage is an ever-deepening connection between a husband and a wife, marked by openness, honesty, forgiveness, grace and perseverance. Intimacy is not the same thing as perfection. A marriage between two selfish people always involves a mix of highs and lows, strengths and weaknesses, successes and failures, joys and pains. The commitment of intimacy allows imperfect people to see beyond the imperfections and to work through the challenges, knowing that a better marriage is often on the other side of those very challenges. God-honoring intimacy relies heavily upon the love we experience in our relationship with Jesus. Once you personally experience the love, grace and forgiveness of Jesus, you have all the necessary tools to work through virtually any barrier to intimacy. I cannot promise that working through challenges will be easy, but it certainly is possible with a proper perspective on Jesus along with a willing effort from you.

Many people simply want intimacy to exist; however, intimacy does not happen accidentally. You must put up a good fight. Fighting for intimacy means working hard to bring your best effort to marriage (even if your spouse does not). Especially in the routine of life, you must fight to remain close.

You must fight to be open and honest.
You must fight to put down your phone.
You must fight to listen and validate.
You must fight to resolve the problem.
You must fight for physical and emotional intimacy.
You must fight to support one another's dreams.
You must fight for a date night.
You must fight to serve each other.
You must fight your selfishness.

Are you ready to fight the good fight for true intimacy?

On the **FIGHT FOR INTIMACY** gauge below, rate your marriage using a scale of 1-10.

FIGHT FOR INTIMACY

Remember, this is your individual assessment. I encourage you to be honest and make any specific notes you would like to include or questions you have in the margin.

DAY 1: "ONENESS"

'For this reason a man will leave his father and mother and be united to his wife, and the two will become one flesh.' So they are no longer two, but one flesh. Therefore what God has joined together, let no one separate.
(Mark 10:7-9)

Whatever you do, do not take marriage advice from someone who is single! I remember a pastor telling me this when I was dating and trying to decide about marriage. Now, as a married man, I wholeheartedly agree, unless of course, that unmarried person is Jesus!

In these verses in Mark 10, Jesus was answering a fairly pointed and hostile question about marriage—more specifically, about divorce. The opponents of Jesus' ministry were trying to discredit Him and make Him look foolish. Jesus was aware of their motives but took on the question anyway. He immediately knew the best way to answer any marriage question was to go back to where it all began. Jesus directed their attention back to the very first marriage, the marriage of Adam and Eve found in Genesis 2. He quoted the portion of the text that speaks to the permanence of marriage and reinforced the basic expectation of marriage that the two shall become one flesh.

Becoming one flesh should be constantly on the radar of your marriage. Our understanding and pursuit of oneness is built upon acknowledging God's work in marriage. Marriage is not simply the commitment of a man and a woman. God is part of the equation. This is why Jesus added His divine words in verse 9, "Therefore what God has joined together, let no one separate." The implication is apparent: Because God joined the two of you together, oneness and intimacy becomes something you must fight for. Your effort in marriage reflects a reverence for God as the One who established marriage.

Jesus did not shy away from the question of divorce. While scripture is clear there are exceptions when divorce is necessary, it is never God's desire to see a marriage He established be torn apart. Jesus reminded the Pharisees then, just as He reminds you today: Your marriage is not entirely yours. God is part of the equation. He joined you together. Your priority is to fight for intimacy.

REFLECT & RESPOND:

1. Based on Mark 10:7-9, list the elements of Jesus' words that indicate the permanence of marriage.

2. What or who is the strongest influence on your marriage right now? If your answer is anything other than God's word, take a moment to make a fresh commitment to allow God to lead you in your marriage.

3. In what ways does your attitude reflect a lack of reverence for God's work in your marriage?

4. List one way you can show effort toward oneness in your marriage today.

5. List your AHA moment from today's reading.

DAY 2 : "LOVE & RESPECT"

However, let each one of you love his wife as himself, and let the wife see that she respects her husband.
(Ephesians 5:33)

The subject of intimacy can often leave you thinking about spontaneous and glamorous examples of romance. Perhaps what comes to mind is a steamy sex scene from a TV drama or the cute, clumsy and coincidental meeting of two long-lost lovers in a romantic comedy. Whether on the big screen or small screen, our cultural view of intimacy can leave you wondering why your marriage is not quite as exciting.

In Ephesians 5, Paul speaks directly into marriage by identifying two basic building blocks for intimacy and oneness in marriage. His words answer some of the disconnect you feel when intimacy is not all you long for it to be in your marriage. You likely know these words by heart, but try not to let the familiarity deceive you. Love and respect are critical components to healthy, God-honoring intimacy.

It often has been said, "In marriage a woman needs and desires love just as a man needs and desires respect." I certainly don't object to this reasoning, especially given the specific way Paul presents them in relationship to each respective spouse; however, in addition, there is a deeper issue. Paul's words attack the selfishness in each respective spouse. Paul's challenge for each husband to love his wife combats the gravitational pull he feels to put himself first and not care for his wife the way he should. Instead, a husband ought to recognize this temptation and in turn activate his love for his wife. Likewise, a wife's calling to respect her husband stands in opposition to her desire to control, discourage or demean her husband. In contrast, she gives respect in his direction, strengthening the marriage.

Giving of love and respect to one another creates a sense of intimacy and strength in your marriage. Real marriage intimacy grows, not simply in the receiving of what you long for from your spouse, but in the internal decision to deny yourself and give your best to your marriage.

REFLECT & RESPOND:

1. What act of love (wife) or respect (husband) do you appreciate and long for most?

2. What act of love (wife) or respect (husband) does your spouse appreciate and long for most?

3. Do you ever find yourself unwilling to give your wife acts of love or your husband respect? If so, why?

4. Marriage strength boils down to giving your best. What fears do you have giving your best, regardless of what your spouse chooses to do?

5. List your AHA moment from today's reading.

DAY 3 : "THE GOOD NO"

For the grace of God has appeared that offers salvation to all people. It teaches us to say "No" to ungodliness and worldly passions, and to live self-controlled, upright and godly lives in this present age, while we wait for the blessed hope—the appearing of the glory of our great God and Savior, Jesus Christ.
(Titus 2:11-13)

Intimacy often is narrowly defined by the sexual relationship. While this is certainly part of the intimacy a couple shares in marriage, it is only one dimension of the multifaceted reality of intimacy. Intimacy is also found in the words, experiences, body language and nonsexual touch you share with one another. Here, in Titus 2, the Apostle Paul presents another dimension of intimacy that is seldom brought to light. I call it, "the good NO."

In this passage, Paul reminds Titus of God's grace, a truth you likely appreciate as well. However, Paul makes it clear that God's grace is more than simply a term referring to God's forgiveness. Grace is a teacher. Grace comes in and instructs us to live. Verse 12 says, "[Grace] teaches us to say "NO" to ungodliness and worldly passions, and to live self-controlled, upright and godly lives in this present age." The same grace that forgives our sin and provides eternal hope is the grace that motivates our obedience and godly living. Grace specifically teaches us to say, "NO."

This "NO" is a very important and very good "NO." This kind of "NO" is one that gives your spouse a greater and greater confidence in your character and creates the optimal environment for greater and greater levels of marital intimacy. You likely can attest to this truth personally. You or someone you know has suffered greatly from failing to heed the teaching of God's grace. They said "YES" to ungodliness and worldly passions and walked away from self-control, upright and godly living. When the good "NO" is absent, intimacy is always damaged. God intends for marital intimacy to be built upon godly character motivated by God's grace.

Choosing the good "NO" means trusting in God enough to provide all you need without violating His word or His ways. Recommit to the good "NO" today as both a response to God's wonderful grace and as a wonderful blessing to your marriage.

REFLECT & RESPOND:

1. Give an example of a good "YES" and a good "NO" in your marriage.

2. What does Paul mean when he refers to grace as a teacher?

3. Andy writes, "God intends for marital intimacy to be built upon godly character motivated by God's grace." Do you agree? Why or why not?

4. What good "NO" do you need to commit to starting today?

5. List your AHA moment from today's reading.

DAY 4 : "JUST KILL THE SPIDERS"

Put to death, therefore, whatever belongs to your earthly nature: sexual immorality, impurity, lust, evil desires and greed, which is idolatry. Because of these, the wrath of God is coming. You used to walk in these ways, in the life you once lived. But now you must also rid yourselves of all such things as these: anger, rage, malice, slander, and filthy language from your lips. Do not lie to each other, since you have taken off your old self with its practices and have put on the new self, which is being renewed in knowledge in the image of its Creator.
(Colossians 3:5-10)

My wife does not get along with spiders. As you know, spiders tend to enjoy the indoors, and this causes a certain amount of stress in my home. My wife has made it unmistakably clear that her desire is for me to eliminate spiders whenever they show themselves in our house. I have tried to explain that spiders actually have some good qualities and not every spider is a deadly threat to our family. Still, she doesn't get along with spiders. The solution is simple—just kill the spiders.

Marriage is not always a simple thing. I often meet with couples who are really struggling. Their issues are numerous, and they both have their strongly held opinions as to what the problem is, as well as the solution. I've learned something over the years. By and large, marriage problems boil down to what Colossians 3 refers to as the "earthly nature" or "the life you once lived." These phrases refer to the manner of life before being born again into a faith relationship with Jesus Christ. The expectation of Christianity is the old life you once lived is replaced by new life in Christ. However, it is not uncommon for the habits of the old life to reappear, even after genuinely being born again.

The habits, thought patterns, attitudes and actions of the old life often plague marriages. When these patterns emerge, they place a strain on the intimacy couples are working toward in marriage. The challenge presented in this passage of scripture is essentially as simple as "just kill the spiders." When the old life makes an appearance, we must not treat it casually. Yes, you are human. No, you are not perfect. No, you will never find perfection in this life. However, if you defend a relapse into your "earthly nature" or "the life you once lived," you only further divide the intimacy of your marriage. There is truly only one acceptable response, "Put to death, therefore, whatever belongs to your earthly nature" and "rid yourselves of all such things." Don't give yourself a free pass to allow your old life to rob your new life in Christ or your intimacy in marriage.

REFLECT & RESPOND:

1. How does Colossians 3:5-10 promote marital intimacy?

2. Describe a personal habit, thought pattern, attitude or action that represents the old life you lived before placing your faith in Christ?

3. When you fail or make a mistake in your marriage, do you tend to confess it or defend yourself?

4. What excuses have you used to defend a relapse into your old life?

5. List your AHA moment from today's reading.

DAY 5 : "PURPOSE IN THE PAIN"

Consider it pure joy, my brothers and sisters, whenever you face trials of many kinds, because you know that the testing of your faith produces perseverance. Let perseverance finish its work so that you may be mature and complete, not lacking anything.
(James 1:2-4)

Marriage is not a prison sentence, but if you talk to some people, you might think that's what they are describing. I think that deep down, we all want marriage to be deeply fulfilling, completely comfortable and indescribably intimate. The truth is, I think this is exactly what God wants as well. Unfortunately, so few couples ever experience this kind of marriage, which begs the question, "Why?"

The obvious answer is staring at you in the mirror every day. You married a sinner and so did your spouse! The only proper expectation of married life is that you will have problems, conflicts, miscommunications, disappointments and trials. Yet, in the midst of all this, God's vision for a marriage that is deeply fulfilling, completely comfortable and indescribably intimate is still firmly in place.

James 1 not only acknowledges the reality that you will face trials, but instructs you to consider them "pure joy." Before you throw this book out of a window, give James a chance. It's no secret that trials are an unwelcome part of life. However, James helps us see the purpose in the pain. Every trial, in life or marriage, serves as a testing ground for your faith. Think of this test not as pass or fail but as a forging process, much like steel is tested in the refining process producing stronger, more durable steel. When your faith is tested, your character is forged. It is in the trials that God produces the character to persevere. In marriage, perseverance is a critical factor. As long as your spouse is imperfect, perseverance will be needed.

It's interesting how this passage concludes, "Let perseverance finish its work so that you may be mature and complete, not lacking anything." Perseverance is part of maturity. It is immature to turn and run when you face a trial in your marriage. God intends to use the trial to strengthen your resolve in marriage to produce a deeply fulfilling, completely comfortable and indescribably intimate connection between you and your spouse over time. Perhaps sometimes, fighting for intimacy means looking beyond the current trial to the better day when your marriage is "mature and complete, not lacking anything."

REFLECT & RESPOND:

1. In general, do you think of your marriage as positive, negative or neutral?

2. Do you agree that perseverance and intimacy are connected? Why or why not?

3. Describe a recent or current trial in your marriage.

4. In light of the trial you have described above, in what way is God leveraging the trial for your own maturity?

5. List your AHA moment from today's reading.

SMALL GROUP LEADER GUIDE DISCUSSION QUESTIONS

Thank you for leading your small group or Sunday school class through The Marriage Dashboard Handbook. This curriculum is designed to work in conjunction with a series of videos you can find at www.marriagedashboard.com. On the following pages, you will find discussion questions that are designed to stimulate conversations in your group or class after watching each week's video segment.

After meeting as a group for the introduction on Session 1, group members have the opportunity to complete the handbook portion on their own between group meetings. Each of the five sections provides the participant with a daily reading and response questions. Each section opens with an introduction to the particular gauge on the dashboard. This introduction can be added to the first reading in each section.

The response questions are designed to help the participant think critically about the topic at hand. Group leaders may find it helpful to ask participants to share portions of their responses during the group time. These responses will give leaders unique and personal insights into how participants are engaging the material.

The curriculum is designed to be completed in as few as six sessions, but may be extended at the discretion of the group.

SESSION 1: INTRODUCTION

The first session is designed to present the overall concept of the Marriage Dashboard. I encourage you to watch the entire Marriage Dashboard video, entitled "Session 1" (18:05). This should help group members know what to expect as they dive into the study in the week to come.

1. Andy says, "People do crazy things when they're in love." What were some of the good "crazy" things your spouse used to do when you were first dating?

2. Some could say that a mediocre marriage sounds way better than a lot of bad marriages that they know. But why is Andy suggesting that mediocrity is a very dangerous place for your marriage?

3. Review the "Assessment Tool" page in the beginning of The Marriage Dashboard Handbook. Prepare your couples to make individual and honest assessments as they progress through the curriculum.

SESSION 2 : START WITH GOD

The second session focuses on the Start with God gauge. I encourage you to watch the video entitled, "Session 2" (3:47). This video is the "Start with God" segment taken from the Session 1 video to simply refresh the group on the topic.

1. Describe the role God plays in your life individually and as a couple.

2. Can you think of a time you completely surrendered a marriage issue to God? What happened?

3. What do you think could happen if you started your day out asking, "God, how do I love and bless my spouse today?"

SESSION 3 : HAVE FUN TOGETHER

The third session focuses on the Have Fun Together gauge.
I encourage you to watch the video entitled, "Session 3" (2:27).
This video is the "Have Fun Together" segment taken from the Session 1 video to simply refresh the group on the topic.

1. Describe the last time you had fun together.

2. List three activities you consider to be fun with your spouse.

3. What do you think is the greatest obstacle to having fun together in your marriage right now?

SESSION 4 : HONOR EACH OTHER

The fourth session focuses on the Honor Each Other gauge.
I encourage you to watch the video entitled, "Session 4" (2:59).
This video is the "Honor Each Other" segment taken from the Session 1 video to simply refresh the group on the topic.

1. How have you observed another couple show dishonor toward one another? (Please don't share names.)

2. What dishonorable behavior or speech have you been guilty of giving your spouse?

3. Is there a specific offense that has become an obstacle to honoring your spouse?

SESSION 5 : LIVE IN COMMUNITY

The fifth session focuses on the Live in Community gauge.
I encourage you to watch the video entitled, "Session 5" (1:22).
This video is the "Live in Community" segment taken from the Session 1 video to simply refresh the group on the topic.

1. Evaluate your five closest friends and your three closest "couple" friends. Are they headed in the same direction you would desire for yourself and your marriage?

2. Do you regularly have conversations with other couples about your marriage and their marriages? Do these conversations tend to stay positive or head in a negative direction quickly?

3. What environments do you engage in together (or need to engage in together) to find healthy community for the good of your marriage?

SESSION 6: FIGHT FOR INTIMACY

The sixth session focuses on the Fight for Intimacy gauge. I encourage you to watch the video entitled, "Session 6" (3:29). This video is the "Fight for Intimacy" segment taken from the Session 1 video to simply refresh the group on the topic.

1. How much "fight" are you bringing to your marriage to stay close and connected?

2. What are some ways you can fight for intimacy other than sexual intimacy?

3. Does the idea of being "fully known and fully loved" excite you or frighten you?

ADDITIONAL RESOURCES FROM ANDY SAVAGE

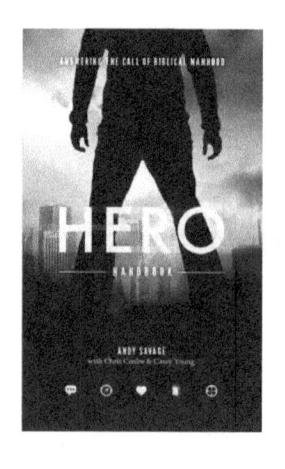

THE HERO HANDBOOK
by Andy Savage
The Hero Handbook is a devotional book just for men to discover God's vision for authentic manhood to be a Hero. Each daily reading is designed to stretch you spiritually and you practically. Don't quit. Stay with it, and watch God transform your life. Whether you are short or tall, young or old, single or married, God wants men to embody and expand the five "character traits of a hero."

GIANT LOVE
by Andy Savage
GIANT LOVE, a fully illustrated book, is a unique resource for parents to help their children understand God's Giant Love. Your kids will be captivated by the story of a little boy who faces the giants of sin and consequence only to discover there is another Giant, the biggest one of all who saves the day! The discussion guide included in this book will help parents lead the way in some of the most important conversations one can have with their child. Every child needs to know about God's Giant Love.

Andy's prayer is to see this book in the hands of thousands of parents who take the opportunity to guide their own children into a relationship with Jesus Christ. This book will also serve as a keepsake marking the date of your child's decision to trust Christ and his or her first steps in the Christian life.

THE ADVENTURES OF COOPER THE TURTLE

Cooper the Turtle will steal your heart the moment you open the book. Andy Savage truly captures the spirit of childhood imagination and adventure. What child hasn't dreamed of flying? What child doesn't wake up each day eager for adventure? Each page is beautifully designed by illustrator Charlie Forrester. Charlie brilliantly depicts the endless fun and wonder of a forest. The imagery will draw you in and make you feel like you are part of the story.

The other animals who have befriended Cooper enthusiastically support his dreams of adventure. This simple story of helping a friend will motivate you to look for ways, both big and small, to help someone you know achieve their dreams. Cooper the Turtle can do anything, with some imagination and a little help from his friends.

The Adventures of Cooper the Turtle was inspired by and dedicated to all the wonderful people in our world with Down syndrome who show us all how to love—the nearest and dearest of whom is Andy's second child, Cooper.

Visit andysavage.com for a complete list of Andy's resources.

OTHER RESOURCES FROM HIGHPOINT CHURCH

PRIORITY TIME BOOK
by Chris Conlee

MISS PERFECT
by Karin Conlee

Visit highpointmemphis.com for a complete list of Highpoint resources.